15 MAY 2022 Developing Parental Involvement
in Primary Schools

3

Developing Parental Involvement in Primary Schools

Roy Long

M

Macmillan Education

First published 1986

Published by
MACMILLAN EDUCATION LTD
Houndmills, Basingstoke, Hampshire RG21 2XS
and London
Companies and representatives
throughout the world

Printed in Hong Kong

British Library Cataloguing in Publication Data
Long, Roy
    Developing parental involvement in primary schools.
    1. Parent-teacher relationships—England
    2. Education, Elementary—England
    I. Title
    372.11'03   LC235.G7

ISBN 0-333-39829-7

Contents

Foreword

Parental involvement in the education of young children poses a considerable challenge to schools and teachers. We know, from reports of numerous initiatives across the country, that it is a challenge which many teachers want to take up. But there are two problems which often arise.

First, which kind of parental involvement should be tried? There is a need to sort out the different kinds which have been developed, and to identify their advantages and disadvantages in the circumstances of a particular school. Second, teachers sometimes need to prepare themselves for a changed professional role. Programmes of initial (and in-service) training rarely try to equip teachers with the outlook or skills needed in working with parents. We need a new approach to training.

This practical guide by Roy Long will be a significant help in overcoming these problems. It is the outcome of some earlier work in school-focused INSET which was evaluated and found to be useful. It provides some information and ideas about possible lines of work with parents but, more importantly, it suggests ways in which teachers can come together, in a workshop setting, to think out what they want to do.

I hope it will be well-used.

Peter Hannon
University of Sheffield

Preface

'Parental involvement' means different things to different people – from parents repairing library books or helping on trips, to parent aides working in the classroom, or giving home-based help with reading – but relatively few schools in Britain can claim to have a considered policy in which parents are meaningfully involved in their own children's learning. Parental involvement can mean so much more than a way of liberating school staff from tedious tasks, so much more than a token home-reading project.

Where parents have become involved in their own children's learning, the children's school performance has invariably improved quite significantly, so there is increasing pressure on schools to respond to this new challenge, which calls into question the traditional role of the teacher and, perhaps, the very nature of early education.

Faced with calls for a broader approach to involving parents, teachers will need to revise old skills, learn new ones and adapt to the emerging demands for fuller collaboration with parents. To make this transition as smooth as possible, and help to ensure that parental involvement programmes in schools have a good chance of success, teachers must be given the opportunity to consider the issues involved, and the implications for them at school level.

This book offers a consideration of some of the important issues, and looks at the range of possible developments. It makes practical suggestions for school-based workshops, so that teachers can fully debate the issues and the problems, and work towards a coordinated programme of parental involvement in their school. Finally, it offers brief reviews of some of the useful reference sources on parental involvement, and a supplementary bibliography. Asterisks in the text denote sources reviewed in Part 3.

'The finest school will be even finer when it acknowledges the powerful contribution of every parent, however much we, as amateur sociologists, might have categorised them as disadvantaged.' (John Coe, Chairperson of the National Association for Primary Education, September 1984)

Part 1:   Involving parents

THE PROCESS OF INVOLVING PARENTS

In many ways, the Plowden Report (CACE, 1967) may be seen as a starting-point in the process of involving parents. Plowden offered a perspective which was effectively 'school-supporting' – persuading parents of the value of the school's work and involving them peripherally in such things as fund-raising and repair work. With the value of hindsight, it is easy to highlight the restrictions and omissions of Plowden. But this is not doing it justice, for Plowden crystallised and initiated some key ideas in the field which, while not radical in themselves, have formed a basis from which current trends have developed. It gave official recognition to the problem of 'good relations' between teachers and parents, which were mainly social, called for positive action and thought from schools on parental involvement, and advocated home-visiting and increased community involvement as strategies to be considered by schools.

While Plowden, albeit tentatively, suggested a 'partnership', little evidence of this was found in nursery schools ten years later (Tizard, 1977). Contacts were found to be social rather than educational. While parents have come into school as helpers, fund-raisers or classroom aides, cooperation in the teaching–learning process has rarely been achieved.

Nonetheless, the process of parental involvement is under way, though the pace may be slow. A survey carried out by the National Foundation for Educational Research found that there has been a post-Plowden move towards increased parental involvement in schools (Cyster, Clift et al., 1980). This study further indicated that there has been an increasing incidence of examples of 'active' cooperation, involving parents more meaningfully in their children's learning.

Recent home-reading projects at Haringey (Hewison, 1981*) and Belfield (Jackson and Hannon, 1981*), and school-based projects at Sheffield (Weinberger, 1983*) and in the Midlands (Rathbone and Graham, 1981*) have pointed the way to a 'collaboration' stage in the process of involvement (fig. 1), where parents are encouraged to become involved in limited specific educational tasks, such as hearing their children read at home. These projects signify an 'official' acceptance of the educative role of the parent.

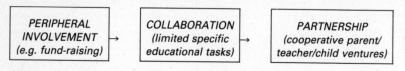

| PERIPHERAL INVOLVEMENT (e.g. fund-raising) | → | COLLABORATION (limited specific educational tasks) | → | PARTNERSHIP (cooperative parent/teacher/child ventures) |

Fig. 1:   *Parental involvement as a three-stage process*

However, even to reach the 'collaboration' stage, let alone move on towards 'partnership', the process of development must take place at two levels. At the school level, a school which still retains a 'no parents beyond this point' ethos is unlikely to pursue a vigorous parental involvement programme on collaborative or partnership lines. At the individual level, the teacher who views the teaching of reading as a particular professional skill is hardly ready to participate in a home-reading project.

Any involvement with parents at the level of partnership must demonstrate the cardinal principle of reciprocity (Wolfendale, 1982*): mutual involvement, mutual accountability, mutual gain and mutual trust. The 'partnership' stage will see the school as a resource centre for the community, and the teacher as a facilitator of children's learning wherever it takes place (Deer, 1980; Woodhead, 1981*).

But while the 'partnership' stage may be the ultimate goal, the aim of any courses or workshops on involving parents must be to 'move' schools or teachers along the continuum from their present stage of development to something to which they can comfortably adapt. Meaningful parental involvement has many implications for teachers and their role in education, and these need to be fully aired and debated if progress is to be consolidated and maintained.

INVOLVING PARENTS – WHY?

Why involve parents? Because it has been proved that parental involvement improves children's school performance, and anything that does so must merit close attention. While evidence is only just beginning to accrue in Britain (for example, Hewison, 1982; Widlake and MacLeod, 1984), there is a large body of evidence from American schools which indicates that, whatever the form of involvement, the effect on children's school performance is positive, provided the involvement is well-planned, comprehensive, and long-lasting, and serves to integrate the child's experiences at home and school (for example, Gillum *et al.*, 1977*; Herman and Yeh, 1980; Fantini, 1980*; Henderson, 1981*).

Why involve parents? Because they are already involved as the primary educators of their children before school or nursery, and it makes sense to continue and utilise this involvement in the early years of formal education. Attention has recently been drawn to the scope for learning in the early years, and the crucial role of the parents. However the state of parenthood as a stage of life, with its own special features and responsibilities, has not yet been properly recognised, nor subjected to any intensive research or study. Even though parents are showing an increasing desire to take some responsibility for their children's early education (e.g. through playgroups, or mother and toddler groups), the status of parenthood remains low (Woodhead, 1981*). Lack of parental interest is often cited as a reason for low educational achievement, but several studies have shown that, given specific tasks and sufficient encouragement and assurance, a good majority of parents from all backgrounds are most anxious to help their children (for example, Rathbone, 1977*; Hewison, 1980; Smith, 1980; Prosser, 1981; Athey, 1981*; Jackson and Hannon, 1981*).

Why involve parents? Because such involvement has positive advantages for children, teachers and parents. By extending the contexts of learning beyond the confines of the classroom and the school, the child finds a wider range of constructive learning situations, the teacher develops his or her professional role as a facilitator of learning wherever it takes place, and the parent gains skills and confidence to extend his or her child's learning.

THE ROLE OF THE TEACHER

The success of any parental involvement venture depends very largely on the attitudes of the teachers putting it into operation (Bedi and Castleberry, 1980*). Having to share professional expertise and 'put it up for scrutiny' calls for a radical reappraisal of traditional attitudes (Prosser, 1981).

For a variety of reasons – historical, institutional and cultural – the involvement of the teacher in early education has tended to drive a 'wedge' between the parent and the child (fig. 2), diminishing the importance and effectiveness of the 'learning bond'. To a greater or lesser extent, the teacher has assumed the central educative role.

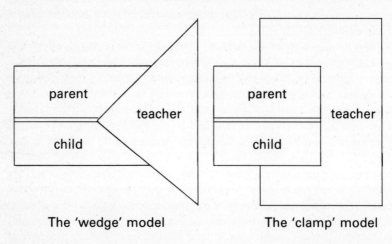

The 'wedge' model   The 'clamp' model

Fig. 2:   *Two models of the teacher's involvement in early childhood education. (The double line represents the parent–child learning bond.)*

With recent developments in communication and information systems in the home, and the problems of coping with the current 'knowledge explosion', the role of the teacher as the expert transmitter of knowledge is becoming outdated. Parents are coming to be seen as part of the solution in education rather than part of the problem (Meighan, 1981*). While studies in the sixties concentrated on the educational needs of the disadvantaged child and the influence of the home on school achievement, the current trend is towards attempting to unite the strengths of parents, child and school in a common effort (Siebert *et al.*, 1979*).

The role of the teacher is moving from an instrumental one ('schools are for teaching kids'), where parental 'deficiencies' need to be remedied, towards a 'community facilitator' dimension, where the school is a resource centre, and the contexts of learning are widened into the home and the community (Deer, 1980). A truly cooperative perspective of early education is founded on a vision which recognises the importance of all the contexts in which a young child learns, be it at home or school, in a park, at the shops, or elsewhere (Woodhead, 1981*).

This 'new' role of the teacher in early education may be crudely conceptualised by the 'clamp' model (fig. 2). In this the teacher recognises the role of the parent as the primary educator of the young child, fosters and develops the parent–child learning bond, and complements the parents' educative role.

The workshops suggested in Part 2 are designed to allow teachers to air their views and express their feelings within a constructive framework through which a realistic programme of parental involvement can be drawn up for each particular school.

INVOLVING PARENTS – HOW?

There are many factors which will influence the development of a school's parental involvement programme: teacher attitudes, previous home–school history, the catchment area, local authority support, and so on. Consequently no two schools will develop the same pattern of involvement.

Generally, parental involvement may be summarised into the following categories:

- (a) involvement of pre-school or nursery parents;
- (b) involvement in school learning processes at home or at school;
- (c) involvement in school support;
- (d) involvement in school government;
- (e) home–school relations.

(a) Involvement of pre-school or nursery parents

A review of a wide range of so-called 'early intervention' programmes (Bronfenbrenner, 1975) shows that when parents are centrally involved in the programme, children can make cognitive gains which are sustained over time. Programmes which place high importance on involving parents directly in activities fostering the child's development are likely to have a constructive effect at any age, but the earlier they are started, and the longer they are continued, the greater the benefit to the child.

One project (Athey, 1981*) involved parents in a 'Social Priority Area' working in the nursery with their own children. The parents were continually drawn into a dialogue about what their children were doing and the possible significance of the behaviour. The children made significant gains in all areas of functioning and these gains were maintained over two years in primary school. The parents not only sustained interest in working with the teacher over a two-year period, but became increasingly skilled and autonomous in recognising the fundamental learning that was taking place.

A language facilitation project in a 'priority' nursery (Rathbone, 1977*) involved parents helping their children in class and also supplementing the programme at home. The 'parent involved' group showed significantly higher gains in language and comprehension tests. The keenness and potential ability of the parents surprised the teachers. The researcher suggests that such parental involvement programmes may create a feeling among teachers of their responsibility for the educational climate in a neighbourhood, and may make a contribution to lessening the inhibiting effect of the school situation on the working-class child. Two other parent-based language development projects (Donachy, 1976*; Beveridge and Jerrams, 1981) showed increased gains with the 'parent-involved' groups.

A different approach with pre-school parents is exemplified by the 'Scope' project (Haigh, 1977), which aimed to strengthen and support the educative skills of mothers through regular support-group meetings, with professional input (e.g. medical, educational) when this was requested.

In America, Dorothy Rich has evolved 'recipes' for parent–child activities which give parents clear, straightforward instructions for using domestic items to help children develop learning skills and good learning habits (Meighan, 1981*; Berger, 1981*; Nedler and McAfee, 1979*).

Obviously, pre-school parents can be involved in many other ways. These examples serve only to indicate the range of possibilities.

(b) Involvement in school learning processes at home or at school

Perhaps the best known example of this type of parental involvement is *home reading*, where parents are encouraged to hear their children read regularly at home. Projects at Haringey and elsewhere have shown that if parents spend about ten minutes daily hearing their child read, the children's reading performance is significantly improved (Hewison and Tizard, 1980; Tizard, Schofield and Hewison, 1982; Hewison, 1982). The children benefit from the extra practice and the extra motivation that comes from knowing that their parents are interested and involved. The parents benefit from increased confidence and self-esteem at being given a valid part to play in their child's learning. Project workers stress the importance of genuine cooperation between parents and teachers, and good support for parents by way of practical tips (fig. 3).

Do:
- find a quiet comfortable place;
- sit close to your child;
- talk about the pictures first;
- read the page to your child if he/she wants you to;
- tell your child any word he/she gets stuck on;
- give lots of praise and encouragement.

Don't:
- make reading a chore;
- put pressure on your child;
- go on too long;
- be afraid to talk things over with the teacher.

Fig. 3:   *A list of 'Do's and 'Don't's for home reading*

Paired reading is a specific technique which has been developed by educational psychologists for use with remedial junior readers (Bushell, Miller and Robson, 1982*). The child chooses the book, and parent and child read aloud together at the child's speed, with regular gestures of approval, the parent offering any word the child cannot manage easily. The child knocks on the table when he or she feels able to manage alone. If the child gets stuck, the parent reads the word and they carry on reading aloud together till the child knocks again. Paired reading has shown how parents can be successfully involved, even at the junior stage, where children are already failing.

Parents can also be involved in school learning processes through *workshop* methods. In a reading workshop at Fox Hill Nursery–First School in Sheffield (Weinberger, 1983*), parents spent an hour a week in class working with their own children on books, games or worksheets, under the supervision of the teacher. Parent workshops can also be run after school to introduce parents to home–school learning activities, or to make games and activities for use at home with children – termed 'Make and Take' workshops (Berger, 1981*).

A language programme for seven- to eight-year-olds was run in one school with the help of parents (Rathbone and Graham, 1981*). Although parents were not specifically working with their own children, the 'parent involved' group showed significantly higher gains than the children who had had the programme as part of their normal curriculum.

The *recipe* approach outlined previously is also suitable for giving parents clear and specific home activities to aid their child's progress in school (Meighan, 1981*; Berger, 1981*; Nedler and McAfee, 1979*).

A further means of involving parents in school learning processes is with a *home–school book*, through which communication between parent and teacher can be maintained, and home activities offered and monitored (Bastiani, 1980).

Many other ways of involving parents in school learning processes can be devised to suit individual situations.

(c) Involvement in school support

'School support' encompasses a wide range of activities which do not directly involve parents' working with their own children (Lyons *et al.*, 1983):

fund-raising – fêtes, Christmas draws, etc.;
direct assistance – repairs to apparatus, toys, books, construction of apparatus, help in the library etc.;
child supervision – trips, visits, parent aides, etc.;
parents as resource teachers – talking to groups about their own expertise – fishing, embroidery, etc.;
social or cultural events – assemblies, festivals, etc.

Some parents may, for various reasons, be 'inaccessible' and not easily reached by the school, and school support activities offer a relatively non-threatening way of getting such parents involved.

Some schools set up a 'parents' room', where parents can socialise in a relaxed atmosphere and work on repair jobs and preparation of materials. This may also become a resource centre for parent activities.

(d) Involvement in school government

Generally, parental involvement in school government is guided by legislation, and the scope for a school to develop its own initiatives in this area is limited.

While the balance of power on school governing bodies may be crucial, it is an issue which is likely to provoke confrontation and polarisation, so it is perhaps an area to be avoided in the context of the present discussion.

(e) Home–school relations

Perhaps this is the most fundamental area of parental involvement. If the relationship is right, and there is a high degree of mutual trust between parent and teacher, there will be an effective flow of information in both directions, and parental involvement projects will have a good chance of success (Lyons *et al.*, 1983).

A wide range of methods can help to promote effective information exchange:

home contacts – visits, phone calls, letters;
school contacts – open days, individual parent–teacher meetings, parent meetings;
parents' room/library;
parent survey/questionnaire – to determine areas of concern, and problems, or evaluate home–school relations;
written communications – posters, calendars of events, class newsletters, school newsletters;
parent handbook – basic information, contacts, suggested home activities;
media announcements – local press, local radio.

It is also possible to promote good relations between parents and teachers through outings, social events and other joint functions.

Schools have an opportunity to offer active leadership and support for parents in developing and deepening their involvement in their children's learning. By setting the right climate, schools can encourage parents to play a key role in early childhood education.

Part 2: Practical suggestions for workshops

SCHOOL-BASED IN-SERVICE TRAINING

If parents are to be successfully involved in the education of their children, teachers must first be convinced that the extra effort and time taken are worthwhile. They must be given the opportunity to explore the issues and express their doubts and reservations freely, otherwise any parental involvement programme will be much less likely to prove satisfying or successful.

One means of raising issues and stimulating debate is to run a school-based in-service course in the school itself. This has four distinct advantages over the traditional centre-based course:

(a) it happens at the workplace;
(b) it involves most, if not all, of the school staff;
(c) school-based INSET (in-service education and training) is more likely to invoke active participation than the more distant, more theoretical centre-based variety;
(d) being at the workplace, the participants become the 'experts', and the provider's role is changed to that of 'facilitator' or 'consultant'.

The James Report stressed the changes in emphasis necessary to encourage innovation in the school itself (DES, 1972, para 2.21):

In-service training should begin in the schools. It is here that learning and teaching take place, curricula and techniques are developed and needs and deficiencies revealed. . . . An active school is constantly reviewing and re-assessing its effectiveness, and is ready to consider new methods, new forms of organisation and new ways of dealing with the problems that arise.

This concept of an 'active' school has implications for the shape and style of in-service provision. The 'active', or 'self-evaluating' school responds to external pressures for change, accepts and considers internal demands for change, and involves all staff in formulating proposals to respond to these pressures or demands (Bolam, 1982). Innovation and change are negotiated through 'learning collectives' which include staff at all levels (Chambers, 1981).

The key role of provider, whether it is filled by the head, an adviser, or some other member of staff, is more that of a coordinator and consultant, rather than an expert. The provider seeks a collaborative effort, coordinating ideas, and structuring discussion and debate.

It is useful to evaluate school-based INSET as it is going on, in order to make the course as relevant as possible to the participants (Long, 1983). Written comments can be sought anonymously at the end of each session, and used to refine and improve succeeding workshops.

THE TEACHER AS LEARNER

If a successful school-based course is to be developed, it is worthwhile considering what contributes to effective adult learning.

Several features have been found to be common to courses which were perceived as successful (Galloway, 1982): attendance is voluntary and participants play some part in planning the course; the provider has some idea of the participants' 'needs and wants', and offers a flexible programme which can be adapted to the participants' needs; participants are actively involved throughout, and have time for informal talk and discussion.

Active involvement is crucial for effective learning – the learning must be matched to the learners' experiences, the learners' contributions must be valued and respected, and the learners must be involved in determining the goals of the learning and how they may be used. Social interaction is an essential feature, not just for effective learning, but to ensure an agreed common ground on which development and change can take place (Ashton, 1982; Knowles, 1977; Pope, 1980).

Several strategies may be employed to help to ensure active involvement of the participants and social interaction in groups of various sizes.

Icebreakers (Berger, 1981*) are short 'light' activities which encourage interaction and, used at the outset of a course, can help to generate a warm, accepting climate and help participants to relax and become involved in the group.

Buzz groups (Berger, 1981*) are small discussion groups of four to six participants meeting for a few minutes with no leader, and reporting back to the wider group. These smaller groups offer a means of involving most people actively.

Brainstorming (Parnes and Meadow, 1959; Beaucham and Borys, 1981) is an effective means of producing ideas quickly for subsequent evaluation. Participants work in small groups to produce as many ideas as possible in a short period of time. A 'scribe' is appointed to note down all offerings. No criticism is allowed, 'crazy' ideas are welcomed, and combinations or adaptations of previous ideas are permitted. Sometimes 'crazy' ideas can be fruitful, since there is less concern for being considered and non-controversial. They are also useful for developing a good climate.

The *chessboard* (Wragg, 1974) is a means of encouraging lateral thinking by setting two sets of parameters along either dimension of a grid, and then choosing a square and 'making it fit'. This is explained in more detail in Workshop 1 below.

Structured wall-charts (Long, 1983) which can be developed as the session progresses form a valuable visual aid and focal point to which all can contribute. Handouts which are copies of the data thus generated are likely to have more relevance and usefulness for the participant than the normal type of handout, and indicate that the participants' contributions are valued.

When instructions are given, it is advisable to check understanding at each stage, so participants are clear about what they are doing. Finally, time must be allowed for *open discussion* at the end of every session, in order that participants can air their views and attitudes, and 'fit' the learning to themselves and their own situations.

In school-based courses, as in others, there is a place for variety and texture – a variety of experiences and approaches which stimulate different responses in the participants and maintain interest and attention (Fisher and Hicks, 1982).

WORKSHOP 1: THE POTENTIAL OF PARENTS AS EDUCATORS

The aim of the first workshop is to reveal how much potential exists for involving parents more directly in their children's education.

After a general introduction to the course, including, if necessary, an 'icebreaker' activity, the participants work in pairs to develop a matrix (displayed as a wall-chart) which can be used to indicate how parents can benefit their child's school performance. By working in pairs in the first session, each participant is actively involved, and material is produced which can be of practical use later.

Workshop 1 in detail

The following wall-charts should be prepared in advance and displayed during the workshop: the blank matrix(fig. 5); the icebreaker poster(s); the course outline (fig. 4); a 'Comments' poster.

Ample supplies of paper and felt-tips should be made available.

General introduction

Scope of course   Refer to course outline (fig. 4). Discuss briefly. (The programme can be adapted or altered as the course proceeds.) Seek agreement for the basic programme outlined.

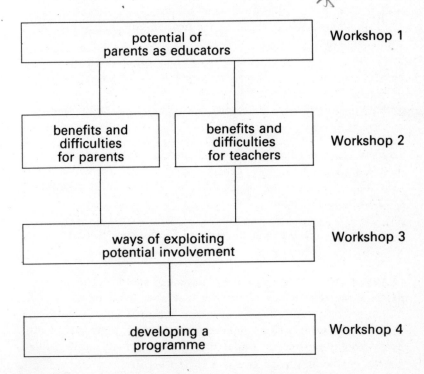

Fig. 4:   *An outline of a possible course on involving parents*

Icebreaker activity   Invite participants to add a comment to a poster entitled: 'Parental involvement is . . .'. Discuss briefly. Or invite comments on two posters: 'Good parent'; 'Bad parent'. Discuss briefly.

The teacher as expert   The workshops operate on 'participant-involved' lines – valuing the expertise of the teacher. Any comments are welcome at any time. The role of the group leader is that of a facilitator: helping to develop and structure the participants' own ideas.

The potential of parents as educators

The participants work in pairs to develop a matrix which indicates how much scope there is for parents to help their children to develop skills useful in school.

Skill areas   In pairs, write down as many skill areas (qualities or skills valued in school) as possible in one to two minutes, e.g. motor skills, number language. Each pair in turn offers a skill area to fill up the matrix (fig. 5).

Parent–child activities   In a similar fashion, develop a list of parent–child activities – activities which parent and child can share, such as shopping, baking – and fill up the other dimension of the matrix.

Using parents' potential   Working in the same pairs for four to five minutes, choose any square on the matrix and, working in any direction across the matrix, generate specific activities which parent and child could share which would help the child develop skills and qualities valued in school.

Report back   Each pair then discusses the list they have developed with the rest of the group.

Open discussion   This part of the workshop should occupy at least a third of the time allocated for the workshop, and might usefully follow a break for coffee. It may be supported by a 'Comments' wall-chart, to which salient points can be added during the discussion. Some questions may be useful to stimulate debate, or get things going:

How could we organise and present these activities?

Are any of these activities class-biased?

Skill areas	Parent–child activities	Baking	Shopping	Gardening	Radio/records	Play/games	Household jobs	Visits	Pets/animals	Television	Library	Hobbies	Sewing	Woodwork
Listening														
Talking														
Spatial awareness														
Role-play														
Auditory skills														
Social skills														
Motor skills														
Language development														
Number language														
Coordination														
Manipulation														
Constructive play														
Imaginative play														
Writing skills														
Observation														
Reading skills														
Confidence														
Self-esteem														
Craft skills														

Fig. 5: *An example of a matrix to show the potential of parents as educators*

How might parents react to being asked to do these activities?
Could parents be involved in drawing up a range of activities – i.e. making up their own matrix?

Evaluation   Seek anonymous written comments on any aspect of the workshop.

WORKSHOP 2: BENEFITS AND DIFFICULTIES OF INVOLVEMENT

The second workshop aims to examine, in a structured way, some of the benefits and difficulties parental involvement might present for teachers and for parents, and to look at how some of these difficulties can be minimised. The participants work in small groups to complete a structured wall-chart.

Workshop 2 in detail

The main wall-chart (fig. 6) and 'Comments' poster should be prepared in advance and displayed during the workshop.

Sufficient large group charts should also be prepared to supply the groups with copies of the following:

'Parents – benefits'; 'Parents – difficulties'; 'Teachers – benefits'; 'Teachers – difficulties'; 'Parents – minimising difficulties' and 'Teachers – minimising difficulties'.

Seating should be organised so that groups of three or four people form naturally.

Introduction   The purpose of this workshop is to examine, in a structured way, some of the benefits and difficulties parental involvement might present for teachers and parents and to look at how some of these difficulties might be minimised.

Brainstorming   This is a useful technique for producing a lot of ideas in a short time. One person in each group is to be 'scribe' – nominated to write down all contributions. The scribe is not a leader. There are three rules:
   (a) no criticism is permitted of ideas offered;
   (b) crazy ideas are welcomed;
   (c) combinations or adaptations of previous ideas are permitted.

Parents – benefits and difficulties   Working in groups of three or four, half of the groups brainstorm on to group charts the following: 'From the parents' point of view, what benefits might parental involvement create?' for two or three minutes. At the same time, the other groups brainstorm: 'From the parents' point of view what difficulties might parental involvement create?' Mount the group charts on the wall, and cluster or focus ideas, transferring them to the main wall-chart.

BENEFITS AND DIFFICULTIES OF PARENTAL INVOLVEMENT

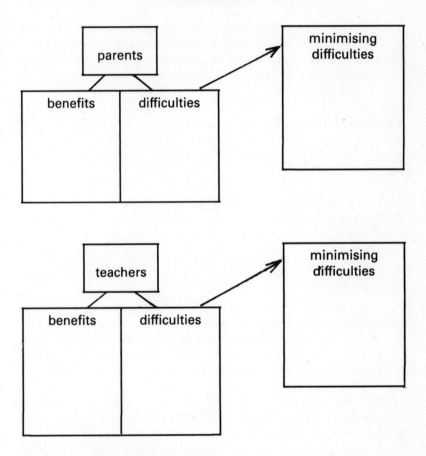

Fig. 6:   *A wall-chart for Workshop 2*

Parents – minimising difficulties   All groups brainstorm the follow-ing: 'How might we, as professionals, minimise the difficulties for parents?' Mount the group charts, and cluster or focus ideas, transfer-ring them to the main wall-chart.

Teachers – benefits and difficulties   In a similar fashion, brainstorm the following: 'From the teachers' point of view, what benefits/difficulties might parental involvement create?' Mount the group charts, and cluster or focus ideas, transferring them to the main wall-chart.

Teachers – minimising difficulties   All groups brainstorm the following: 'How might the difficulties for teachers be minimised?' Mount the group charts, and cluster or focus ideas, transferring them to the main wall-chart.

Open discussion   Again this may be supported by a 'Comments' wall-chart. It may be appropriate to point out that these course methods could be applied to meetings of parents, so parents could actually help develop the parental involvement programme for the school.

Evaluation   Seek anonymous written comments on any aspect of the workshop.

WORKSHOP 3: A CONSIDERATION OF INVOLVEMENT SCHEMES

In finding ways of exploiting the potential of parents as educators, the aim of Workshop 3 is to consider several schemes of parental involvement, and attempt to 'fit' them to the participants' own situation in their school. For example, a group may look at the salient points of a home-reading project, and decide how it might be implemented in that particular school.

The participants work in 'buzz groups', each considering a different scheme of involvement, and how it might be adapted to the situation in their school.

No more than three schemes should be studied in one session, so the most appropriate schemes could be selected for consideration, or Workshop 3 could be extended to two or more sessions if all the schemes are to be considered.

Workshop 3 in detail

Appropriate wall-charts selected from figs 7,9,11,13 and 15 should be prepared in advance and displayed during the workshop. A wall-chart of 'Do's and 'Don't's (fig. 3) should also be displayed.

Group charts (figs 8, 10, 12, 14, 16) should be prepared and displayed to match the selected wall-charts, and seating arranged so

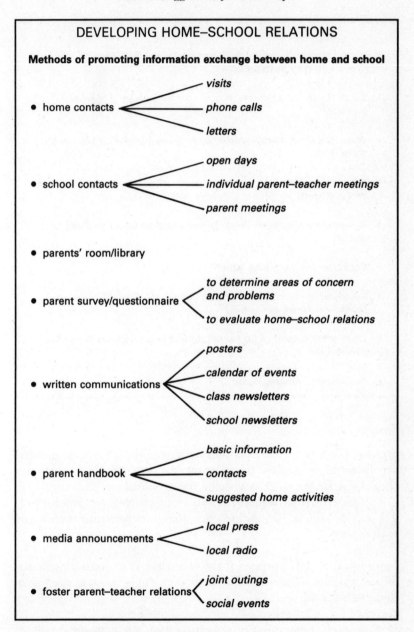

Fig. 7: *A wall-chart for Workshop 3*

DEVELOPING HOME–SCHOOL RELATIONS

- Is our range of home contacts and school contacts wide enough? How could they be improved?

- Could we set up a parents' room/area? Should we? For what purpose?

- Would a parent survey/questionnaire serve a useful purpose in our school?

- Is our range of written communications extensive enough? Could it be developed?

- Is the parent handbook up-to-date and useful? Could anything be added?

- Could we use the media better?

- Could parent–teacher relations be improved? How might we, as professionals, set about this?

- What other aspects of home–school relations might we think about developing?

- Any other comments, ideas . . . ?

Fig. 8:   *A group chart for Workshop 3*

groups of four to six can each consider one of the schemes of parental involvement on display. If a 'Comments' poster is to be used, this should also be prepared in advance and mounted.

The detail on these wall–charts and group charts is not prescriptive, and can be altered or clarified according to particular needs and requirements.

Introduction   The purpose of the workshop is to consider schemes of parental involvement, and see how they might work in practice in this particular school.

Wall-charts   Refer to the wall–charts and run through details of those selected for that session, checking understanding, but avoiding great detail.

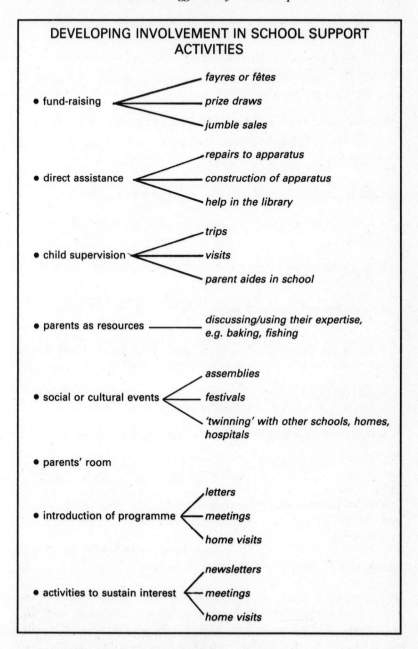

DEVELOPING INVOLVEMENT IN SCHOOL SUPPORT ACTIVITIES

- fund-raising
  - fayres or fêtes
  - prize draws
  - jumble sales

- direct assistance
  - repairs to apparatus
  - construction of apparatus
  - help in the library

- child supervision
  - trips
  - visits
  - parent aides in school

- parents as resources
  - discussing/using their expertise, e.g. baking, fishing

- social or cultural events
  - assemblies
  - festivals
  - 'twinning' with other schools, homes, hospitals

- parents' room

- introduction of programme
  - letters
  - meetings
  - home visits

- activities to sustain interest
  - newsletters
  - meetings
  - home visits

Fig. 9: *A wall-chart for Workshop 3*

DEVELOPING INVOLVEMENT IN SCHOOL SUPPORT ACTIVITIES

- Do we involve parents enough in fund-raising activities? Could we develop their role in fund-raising?

- Could parents usefully become more involved in repairing or making apparatus? How? Where?

- Could parents help more in the library?

- Could parents help more with supervision on trips or visits?

- Could we use parent aides more, both in and out of the classroom? How?

- Do we adequately use parents' skills or expertise in school? Could we develop this aspect of involvement?

- Could we make more of social or cultural events, and widen our involvement in the community?

- Would it be desirable to set aside a parents' room/area where parents could socialise, or engage in school support activities?

- How would we introduce a programme of school support activities to parents? Could/should we involve parents in its development?

- How could we sustain interest in a school support programme?

- Any other comments, ideas . . . ?

Fig. 10:   *A group chart for Workshop 3*

Group charts   Refer to the group charts, which help to offer a structured consideration of the schemes in question.

Buzz groups   Working in discussion groups with a scribe but no leader, each group selects a scheme of parental involvement from the wall-charts, and discusses how such a scheme might work in the school, using the group chart provided as a structured guide. The discussions should last for fifteen to thirty minutes.

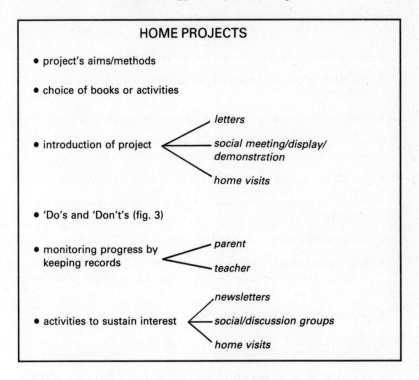

HOME PROJECTS

- project's aims/methods

- choice of books or activities

- introduction of project
  - letters
  - social meeting/display/demonstration
  - home visits

- 'Do's and 'Don't's (fig. 3)

- monitoring progress by keeping records
  - parent
  - teacher

- activities to sustain interest
  - newsletters
  - social/discussion groups
  - home visits

Fig. 11: *A wall-chart for projects such as home reading, paired reading or home activity books or cards (Workshop 3)*

Report back Mount the group charts on the wall. Each group then discusses its findings with the other participants.

Open discussion This may be supported by a 'Comments' wall-poster as before.

Evaluation Seek anonymous written comments on any aspect of the workshop.

WORKSHOP 4: DEVELOPING A PROGRAMME OF INVOLVEMENT

The aim of Workshop 4 is to help to develop a programme of parental involvement to suit any particular school.

HOME PROJECTS

- What are the aims of the project and methods to be used?

- How will the activities and material be chosen? Who will make the choices?

- Should a pilot project be tried with one class or group? Which?

- How might the project be introduced to reach as many parents as possible? At what stage could parents become involved?

- How should parents be introduced to the techniques involved?

- How much parent involvement is hoped for, in terms of time and frequency?

- How important are the 'Do's and 'Don't's?

- How should progress be monitored? What information should be recorded by: (a) parents; (b) teachers? How best might this recording be done?

- How could interest in the project be sustained once it is in progress?

- Any other comments, ideas . . . ?

Fig. 12:   *A group chart for projects such as home reading, paired reading or home activity books or cards (Workshop 3)*

In buzz groups, the participants consider three aspects of a parental involvement programme:

(a) planning and preparation;
(b) introduction;
(c) maintenance.

After reporting back their findings, the groups come together in plenary session to formulate a timetable for the programme, and consider future needs.

Workshop 4 in detail

If possible, the wall-charts from previous workshops should be on display. In any case, handouts which are copies of the data generated from the previous workshops should be prepared and distributed to all participants.

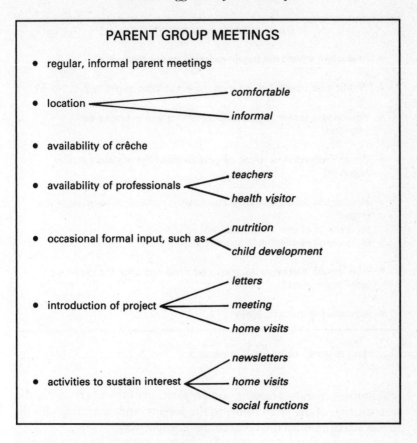

PARENT GROUP MEETINGS

- regular, informal parent meetings

- location — *comfortable*
  informal

- availability of crèche

- availability of professionals — *teachers*
  health visitor

- occasional formal input, such as — *nutrition*
  child development

- introduction of project — *letters*
  meeting
  home visits

- activities to sustain interest — *newsletters*
  home visits
  social functions

Fig. 13: *A wall-chart for Workshop 3*

Group charts on planning and preparation, introduction, and maintenance of a programme (figs 17–19) should be prepared in advance and mounted on a wall. Seating should be arranged so that three groups of four to six form naturally.

A wall-chart on 'Timetable for a programme of parental involvement' (fig. 20) should be prepared in advance, and displayed on the wall, as should a 'Comments' poster, if required.

As before, the detail on these charts is only meant as a guide, and can be changed or clarified according to requirements.

Introduction The aim of Workshop 4 is to prepare a timetable for a programme of parental involvement, taking into consideration the

---

PARENT GROUP MEETINGS

- How often should the parent group(s) meet? Where?

- Would it be possible to arrange a crêche? Who might help to run it?

- How would access to professional advice and guidance be provided?

- Which professionals might be prepared to offer the more formal sessions?

- How would the following be encouraged to become involved in the project:
  (a) parents of pre-school children;
  (b) parents of children in school?

- How would interest in the group be sustained once the meetings were in progress?

- Any other comments, ideas . . . ?

Fig. 14:   *A group chart for Workshop 3*

requirements for the planning and preparation of the programme, the introduction of the programme to the parents, and sustaining interest in the activities once the programme is under way.

Group charts   Refer to the group charts, which help to offer a structured consideration of three aspects of developing a programme of parental involvement. Run through the detail of the charts briefly, then remove them from the wall and give them to the groups.

Buzz groups   Three discussion groups – buzz groups – with a scribe but no leader, will each consider one of the following aspects of the programme of parental involvement:

(a) planning and preparation;
(b) introduction;
(c) maintenance (sustaining interest).

The discussions should last for fifteen to twenty minutes.

PARENT WORKSHOPS

Reading workshops

- parent and child working together under teacher supervision
- 'library' system of home borrowing

'Make and Take' workshops

- parents (without children) make apparatus at school for use at home, e.g. word ladders
- resources must be available: card, glue, staples, etc.
- exchange games, build up stock

General

- introduction of project
  - letters
  - meetings
  - home visits

- monitoring progress by keeping records
  - teacher
  - parent

- availability of crêche

- activities to sustain interest
  - newsletters
  - social functions
  - home visits

Fig. 15: *A wall-chart for Workshop 3*

Report back Mount the group charts on the wall again. Each group then discusses its findings with the others.

Timetable In plenary session, discuss the formulation of a time-table for the programme, referring to the wall-chart. Assign responsibility for various aspects of the programme, and consider any further needs.

PARENT WORKSHOPS

Reading workshops

- When, where, and for how long should the workshop take place?

- How should the material and apparatus be developed?

'Make and Take' workshops

- When, where, and for how long should the workshop take place?

- Could parents help to develop materials?

- How should funds be raised for resources for the workshops?

General

- Should a pilot project be tried with a class or group? Which?

- How might workshops be introduced to reach as many parents as possible?

- What form of records should be kept?

- Could a crêche be organised? Who might help run it?

- How could interest in the workshops be sustained once they are in progress?

- Any other comments, ideas . . . ?

Fig. 16:   *A group chart for Workshop 3*

Open discussion   Again, the discussion element of the workshop may be supported by a 'Comments' wall-poster, and should occupy at least a third of the time allocated for the workshop.

Evaluation   Seek anonymous written comments on any aspects of any of the workshops.

After Workshop 4, handouts of the data generated, including the timetable, should be distributed, so that each participant has copies of all the data generated during the course.

PLANNING AND PREPARING FOR A PROGRAMME OF PARENTAL INVOLVEMENT

- From previous workshops, how can we further develop home–school relations?

- From previous workshops, how can we further develop school support activities?

- From previous workshops, which schemes of parental involvement would we like to introduce in this school?

- Could parents be involved in the planning and preparation stage of these schemes? How?

- What resources or materials will be needed to prepare adequately for the programme?

- Any other considerations . . . ?

Fig. 17: *A group chart for Workshop 4*

INTRODUCING A PROGRAMME OF PARENTAL INVOLVEMENT TO PARENTS

- From previous workshops, how should we introduce our parental involvement programme to the parents?

- How might we reach the 'inaccessible' parents?

- Could parents be involved at the introduction stage? How?

- What resources or materials will be needed to introduce the programme?

- Any other considerations . . . ?

Fig. 18: *A group chart for Workshop 4*

MAINTENANCE OF A PROGRAMME OF PARENTAL INVOLVEMENT

- From previous workshops, how can interest in the parental involvement activities be sustained?

- Could parents be involved in sustaining interest in the activities? How?

- What resources or materials will be needed to sustain interest in the programme?

- Any other considerations . . . ?

Fig. 19:   *A group chart for Workshop 4*

TIMETABLE FOR A PROGRAMME OF PARENTAL INVOLVEMENT

- Could we outline a timetable for the planning and introduction stages of the various aspects of the programme?

SEP		OCT		NOV		DEC	
JAN		FEB		MAR		APR	
MAY		JUN		JLY		AUG	

- Who will be responsible for:
    - (a) coordinating the development of home–school relations and school support activities;
    - (b) the preparation and planning of the selected parental involvement schemes;
    - (c) the introduction of the programme to the parents;
    - (d) the maintenance of the programme?

- What further meetings are necessary?

- Any other considerations . . . ?

Fig. 20:   *A wall-chart for Workshop 4*

Part 3:   Useful reference sources

The literature on parental involvement is expanding fast, as more interest is shown in the subject in Britain. In the USA, however, much has been published since the late sixties/early seventies, and parental involvement is more an established part of the educational scene.

The following reviews summarise many of the experiments and projects carried out in Britain in recent years and discuss a selection of the American literature. This section cannot claim to be comprehensive, but it does offer an introduction to many facets of the subject, both practical and otherwise, and a 'way in' to the literature on parental involvement.

Resources in Education (below) is a journal normally found in university libraries, giving abstracts of report papers and the like. Copies of the originals can be obtained from the USA on microfiche or paper if required, and details of the procedure are in the journal.

REVIEWS

C. Athey, 'Parental involvement in nursery education', *Early Child Development and Care*, 7 (1981) (4) pp. 353–67.

After a short discussion on the quality of adult–child interactions in nursery schools and classes, a brief account is given of a project at the Froebel Educational Institute (1973–8) which aimed at describing, documenting, summarising and finding commonalities and continuities in the behaviour of 20 pre-school children who attended a nursery at the Institute with their parents for three hours a day over a two-year period.

Although there is a lack of data or reference to it in the article, the children (from low socio-economic groups) are claimed to have made outstanding gains in all areas of functioning tested by the standardised tests, which were maintained over two years in the primary school.

Athey argues that because the parents were centrally involved in finding out about their own children, becoming increasingly skilled and autonomous in recognising the fundamental learning that was going on, they were more able, and more willing to support their children's learning: 'Nothing gets under a parent's skin more quickly and more permanently than the illumination of his or her own child's behaviour.'

S. S. Bedi and M. S. Castleberry, 'School – parents – community: a partnership that's working for children', *New Era*, 61 (1980) (1) pp. 17–20.

This article describes a project at an elementary school in Maryland, USA, where the parents are encouraged to participate in the life of the school.

Teachers, parents, and other members of the community worked together in seven areas: school administration; educational programmes; multicultural education; health, nutrition and social service resources; mainstreaming; training; and parent involvement. A wide range of different types of parent involvement developed through the project.

S. Belton and C. Terborgh, *Sparks – Activities to Help Children Learn at Home* (Washington: Human Sciences Press, 1972, reprinted 1976)

A very practical book indicating specific activities to help children learn at home, in a clear, simple format. The home activities are organised under the following headings: reading and language; mathematics; science; art; things to do in the kitchen; things to do while shopping; things to do when travelling.

E. H. Berger, *Parents as Partners in Education: the School and Home Working Together* (UK: Year Book Medical; St Louis, USA: Mosby, 1981)

A comprehensive text-book of parental involvement which gives a great amount of detail and background to many strategies and techniques of parental involvement in the USA.

Deals with many issues relevant to the development of parental involvement in Britain, both practical and theoretical, including parent–child activity sheets, 'Make and Take' parent workshops, communication techniques, ideas for parent meetings, school-based programmes, and many more.

R. Bushell, A. Miller and D. Robson, 'Parents as remedial teachers', *Association of Educational Psychologists Journal*, 5 (Summer 1982) (9) pp. 7–13.

Describes a paired-reading project run by educational psychologists in three schools with a small number of nine- to eleven-year-olds with acute or chronic reading difficulties.

At a meeting in school, parents were shown the techniques by role-play, and given a written synopsis of the technique of reading together. Similarly, at a second meeting, reading independently was taught.

The project itself lasted eight weeks. Parents were asked to read with their child for twenty minutes each night for six nights a week. Home visits were carried out fortnightly by the psychologists to observe the technique in practice.

Though there was no control group, the children on the project made significant gains in accuracy and comprehension, and developed a renewed enthusiasm for books.

W. Donachy, 'Parent participation in pre-school education', *British Journal of Educational Psychology*, 46 (Feb. 1976) (1) pp. 31–9.

A group of pre-school children who received a four-month programme administered by mothers at home were compared with matched control groups. The parent programme was organised through the local primary school or nursery, and after meeting in groups chaired by teachers, each mother chose a library book and was provided with a programme of activities dealing with general vocabulary, simple number and relationships of time, space and size.

Children receiving the parent programme made significant gains on the Stanford-Binet (SB) and Reynell Developmental Language Scales (RDLS). Children attending nursery with no parent programme made significant gains on SB, but not on the RDLS. Children receiving no intervention of any sort did not make significant gains on either test.

Benefits were also noted through a positive improvement in teacher–parent relationships by pursuing a cooperative venture.

M. D. Fantini, 'Community participation: alternative patterns and their consequences on educational achievement', *Resources in Education* (1980) ED 191 167 (Abstract)

A member of the community may become involved in schools as a client, as a resource, as a consumer, or as a decision-maker. Parents can be involved in instruction or in school governance.

Participation in governance seems to show less impact on achievement than involvement in instruction, although further research is called for.

R. M. Gillum *et al.*, 'The effects of parental involvement on student achievement in three Michigan Performance Contracting Programmes', *Resources in Education* (1977) ED 144 007 (Abstract)

The reading progress of seven- to eleven-year-olds involved in a performance contracting programme was tested, using the Stamford Achievement Test and the Metropolitan Achievement Test. Different parental involvement components were involved in these programmes, and student achievement was significantly higher than predicted. Where parents participated in deciding what was taught and had responsibility for working with the teachers and children, achievement was greater than where parental involvement was restricted to filling in forms or attending large group meetings.

A. Granowsky, F. R. Middleton and J. H. Mumford, 'Parents as partners in education', *The Reading Teacher* 32 (1979) (7) pp. 826–30.

Many doubts and fears are raised by parent-involvement programmes. Some of the fears include:

(a) parents will not come to school;
(b) parents do not want to be involved in their children's learning;
(c) teachers do not communicate in ways that parents can understand;
(d) educators do not want parents 'interfering'.

The authors offer their experiences and procedures learned from running a parental involvement programme in Dallas, Texas.
They stress that such programmes are not designed to remove responsibility from the educators, rather that this should be extended beyond the bounds of the classroom and the school. How much a child develops in learning and self-esteem depends to a large extent on how well parents and teachers work together.

A. Henderson (ed.), 'Parent participation – student achievement: the evidence grows', *Resources in Education* (1981) ED 209 754 (Abstract)

This paper reviews evidence from 37 research reports on the effect of parental involvement on student achievement in the USA.

Henderson concludes that the type of parental involvement, whether in or out of school, is not important, provided the involvement is well-planned, comprehensive, and prolonged, and serves to integrate home and school experiences.

J. Hewison, 'Home is where the help is', *Times Educational Supplement* (16 Jan. 1981) pp. 20–1.

This article describes the Haringey Reading Project, which was designed to examine the effect on reading standards in schools of a policy of active parental involvement.

The project took place in six multi-ethnic inner-city schools where reading standards were well below the national average (two experimental schools and four control schools). It ran for two years, covering final year infants and first year juniors (six- to eight-year-olds).

Reading material was chosen by the schools – either scheme readers, a mixture of scheme readers, or supplementary readers and library books. At the minimum, books were taken home every other night.

Home visits were made by one of the researchers two or three times a term, and while no specific instructions were given, demonstrations of 'good practice' were offered as necessary.

At the end of the project, the children who had received help from their parents showed significant gains in reading performance when compared with the control group.

One year after the project, children who had received parental help had maintained their lead in one school, while in the other, the lead had narrowed.

D. J. Irvine *et al.*, 'Parent involvement affects children's cognitive growth', *Resources in Education* (1979) ED 176 893 (Abstract)

Parent involvement in this study included involvement in a pre-kindergarten programme, school visits, home visits by school staff, group meetings and incidental contacts (e.g. telephone calls).

Three kinds of cognitive development were measured:

(a) general reasoning (Walker Readiness Test for Disadvantaged Children);
(b) school-related knowledge and skills (Cooperative Pre-school Inventory);
(c) knowledge of verbal concepts (Peabody Picture Vocabulary Test).

Results showed that parental involvement had a positive effect on all three kinds of cognitive development, regardless of the child's age, mother's education, or family income.

B. K. Iverson *et al.*, 'Parent–teacher contacts and student learning', *Journal of Educational Research*, 74 (1981) (6) pp. 394–6.

This study looks at the effects of teacher–parent contacts on the reading achievement of a large group of under-achievers in an American elementary school district.

For younger children, increasing teacher–parent contacts caused significant gains in reading (measured by the California Achievement Test). However, in older children (twelve- to thirteen-year-olds), increasing numbers of contacts were associated with decreased achievement.

A. Jackson and P. Hannon, *The Belfield Reading Project* (Rochdale: Belfield Community Council, 1981)

A detailed practical account of a home-reading project in a 'community' primary school on a council estate in Rochdale, this booklet sets out clearly and concisely details of how the project was started, and how it developed.

Examples are given of reading cards used, letters sent, record sheets, and a very useful set of 'Do's and 'Don't's for home reading.

Teachers' comments and parents' comments are included, as well as a section on the research involved in the project.

R. Meighan, 'A new teaching force? Some issues raised by seeing parents as educators and the implications for teacher education', *Educational Review*, 33 (1981) (2) pp. 133–42.

The possibility is discussed that parents, instead of being part of the problem in education, may be part of the solution, and various home-teaching strategies are described. This new perspective is set against a changing social context of expanding information systems, the knowledge explosion, the collapse of work, and educational developments such as the Open University. The consequences for teacher education and the changing role of the teacher are critically discussed in relation to the demands of working in a range of cooperative partnerships with parents.

S. E. Nedler and O. D. McAfee, *Working with Parents: Guidelines for Early Childhood and Elementary Teachers* (Belmont, California: Wadsworth, 1979)

A basic text on parental involvement which gives a lot of detail and many examples of schemes and programmes in the USA.

Describes how to implement home-based and school-based parental involvement programmes and looks at establishing an effective home–school partnership. Also discusses how to maintain involvement once a programme is under way.

J. Raim, 'Who learns when parents teach children?' *Reading Teacher*, 34 (1980) (2) pp. 152–5.

A group of 'inner-city' parents assumed a new role – teaching their children school-related skills – and reported improvement in their own reading.

This highlights how the 'urban parent', often with minimal education, can learn to be and feel effective, and perhaps avoid being alienated from the education system.

Results for the children were marginally positive, though their teachers reported improved classroom motivation.

M. Rathbone, 'Parent participation in the pre-school', *Educational Studies*, 3 (March 1977) pp. 81–5.

A group of pre-school children received a ten-week 'language facilitation' programme with the help of their parents in a 'priority' nursery. The parents were also given material and support to continue language development work at home.

A control group who received the ten-week programme in nursery without their parents' help, or any extra help at home, made significantly lower gains on the English Picture Vocabulary Test and the Sentence Comprehension Test than the experimental group.

The teachers were surprised at the enthusiasm and potential abilities of the participating parents.

M. Rathbone and N. C. Graham, 'Parent participation in the primary school', *Educational Studies*, 7 (1981) (2) pp.145–50.

A group of fifteen randomly selected first-year junior children from a working-class area of the Black Country showed significantly higher gains on the English Picture Vocabulary Test and the Daniels, and Diack Reading Test 1 when subjected to a specific language programme implemented by parents in the school, compared to a control and a placebo group. The control group had the same programme as part of their normal curriculum, and the placebo group did number work with a group of parents.

The parents were chosen from those who had been involved for at least four terms in a scheme of parental involvement in the school nursery, and were randomly assigned to groups of three children.

S. and D. Reichert, 'Partners in education – what's realistic?' *Momentum*, 11 (1980) (2) pp. 8–9.

The authors re-examine the relationship that should exist between professional educators, parents and the family to create the effective partnership required for the child.

They identify four principles as a basis for discussion of effective school–home partnerships:

(a) professional educators should clarify their precise roles in the overall education of the child and communicate these to parents;
(b) the school and the professional educator should clarify their expectations of parents in the overall education of the child and communicate these expectations to parents;
(c) together with parents ways should be identified in which the school and teacher can help parents in their responsibility as primary educators;
(d) individual teachers should, as much as possible, personalise their relationships with the parents of the children they teach.

R. B. Rutherford and E. Edgar, *Teachers and Parents: a Guide to Interaction and Cooperation* (Allyn and Bacon, 1979)

Rutherford and Edgar stipulate two basic prerequisites for developing teacher–parent relationships:

(a) teachers must believe that parents have a role in the educational process;
(b) teachers and parents must trust each other.

Various means of exchanging information between parents and teachers are discussed, and teacher–parent cooperation is considered in some detail.

Three specific techniques for solving children's problems and for developing interpersonal skills are examined:

(a) applied behaviour analysis;
(b) interpersonal communication;
(c) assertiveness;

and the process of values clarification is outlined.

L. Sharpe, *Parent–School Relations: a Reconceptualisation* (Sussex University: D. Phil. thesis, 1980)

In a sociological reappraisal of parent–school relations in a comprehensive school, Sharpe discards the 'hidden hand' model of parent–school relations, where parental influence is defined as operating through the child, and there is an innate assumption that teachers' perspectives are correct and normative, and that cooperation is something for parents to do.

In its place, Sharpe develops a model for home–school relations which takes account of the differentiation function of schools in our society, and considers factors such as informal group pressures, latent culture, child–parent relationships, teacher official and unofficial accounts, and social class.

Although the work was done in a comprehensive school, Sharpe's model of home–school relations has obvious implications for early childhood education which are not always prominently featured in such parental involvement studies.

J. B. Siebert *et al.*, 'Emerging trends in parent–school communication', *Resources in Education* (1979) ED 182 734 (Abstract)

A review of research on home–school communication shows that, while studies in the sixties concentrated on the educational needs of the disadvantaged child and the influence of the home on school achievement, the current trend is towards attempting to unite the strengths of parents, child and school in a common effort.

A survey of parents indicated that individual parent–teacher meetings were felt to be the most effective means of communication, followed by open days, reports and notes from teachers.

A. Steller and D. Knox, 'How to develop positive teacher–parent relationships', *Journal of Educational Communication*, 5 (1981) (2) pp. 28–31.

Steller and Knox discuss the problem of teachers' defensive attitudes, which inhibit school–community relations generally and, more specifically, teacher–parent relations. As a remedy, they suggest the development of interpersonal communication skills and specific techniques for home visits and parent–teacher contact through in-service training. They make 28 suggestions to enable heads and administrators to identify the extent of the problem and to reduce teachers' defensive attitudes towards the public.

H. T. Suchara, 'Parents and teachers: a partnership', *Childhood Education*, 58 (1982) (3) pp. 130–3.

A preliminary discussion emphasises the complexity of relationships among parents, teachers and children and the need for systematic building of confidence and competence in the home–school partnership.

In order to advance the concept of partnership, Suchara offers ideas and suggestions for administrators, heads and teachers wanting to build and sustain a meaningful alliance with parents. Useful suggestions for teachers include parents' tables or bulletin boards, class newsletters, seasonal activity lists and lists of local visits. ·

J. M. Trezza, 'Reading for sale!' *Resources in Education* (1982) ED 225 138 (Abstract)

This paper offers a range of imaginative approaches to inform parents about the importance of reading and to motivate cooperation:

(a) a column in the local newspaper;
(b) 'Make and Take' parent workshops, where parents come to school and make reading games for home use;
(c) a one-week 'Parents as Reading Partners' programme in elementary schools;
(d) a school 'Book Swap 'n' Shop' where children can exchange used books.

By working with, and reaching parents, the schools involved have been able to reach more children and improve reading test scores.

J. Weinberger, *Fox Hill Reading Workshop* (London: Family Service Unit Publications, 1983)

This report describes a reading workshop in Fox Hill Nursery–First

School in Sheffield, where parents were involved in helping their children with reading in school for an hour a week.

Details are given on research methods and results, and there is a very useful section on games used and developed at the workshop.

J. Weinberger and P. Hannon, 'Do reading workshops work?' *Times Educational Supplement* (15 July 1983) p. 17.

This article summarises the setting up of a regular reading workshop in Fox Hill Nursery–First School in Sheffield, where parents and teachers worked together on the activities used to teach reading in the school.

A part-time adult-education worker was provided by the voluntary social-work agency, Family Service Units, and the parents of 24 five- to six-year-olds were invited into school to work with their own children for an hour each week.

Such was the success of the experiment that the school continued the workshop without outside help and extended it to cover more teachers and pupils.

S. Wolfendale, 'Parents – clients or partners?' *Association of Educational Psychologists Journal*, 5 (1982) (10) pp. 47–9.

While there has been a post-Plowden move to increased parental involvement in schools, this has not been significantly on partnership lines.

Wolfendale suggests a policy for partnership: abandoning the 'client concept', consulting parents in the same way as professionals, centrally involving parents in the educational processes and assuming mutual responsibility for outcomes.

A cardinal principle of reciprocity should operate: mutual involvement, mutual accountability, mutual gain.

M. Woodhead, 'Cooperation in early education – what does it mean? Why does it matter?' *Early Child Development and Care*, 7 (1981) (2 and 3) pp. 235–52.

While cooperation between parents and professionals may be desirable, the lack of precision in such terms as 'parent participation', 'parent involvement', or 'parent–teacher partnership' is discussed, followed by an analysis of the changing relationship between professionals and parents in early education. The notion that the educational role of the family is diminishing is critically evaluated, and Woodhead argues for a new emphasis on the educational importance of parenthood, and a concept of early education based on cooperation, recognising the value of learning wherever it happens, with the teacher as a facilitator of this process.

BIBLIOGRAPHY

F. Ashton, 'Teacher education: a critical view of skills training', *British Journal of In-Service Education*, 8 (1982) (3) pp. 160–7.

J. Bastiani, 'Bridging the gap between home and school', *Where*, 155 (Feb. 1980) pp. 12–13.

L. Beaucham and A. Borys, 'A strategy for uncovering teacher professional development needs', *British Journal of In-Service Education*, 8 (1981) (1) pp. 19–21.

M. Beveridge and A. Jerrams, 'Parental involvement in language development – an evaluation of a school-based parental assistance plan', *British Journal of Educational Psychology*, 51 (Nov. 1981) pp. 259–69.

R. Bolam, *School-focused INSET* (London: Heinneman Educational, 1982)

U. Bronfenbrenner, *A report on longitudinal evaluations of pre-school programmes*, vol. 2, *Is early intervention effective?* (Washington DC: DHEW Publ., 1975): summary in U. Bronfenbrenner and M. A. Mahoney, *Influences on human development*, second edition (Hinsdale, Illinois: Dryden Press, 1975)

Central Advisory Council for Education, *Children and their Primary Schools*, vol. 1 (Plowden Report) (London: HMSO, 1967)

J. Chambers, 'Staff development – decision-making and contracts', *British Journal of In-Service Education*, 8 (1981) (1) pp. 14–18.

R. Cyster, P. Clift *et al.*, *Parental Involvement in Primary Schools* (Slough: NFER, 1980)

C. Deer, 'Research on school–community relations in Australia', *New Era*, 61 (1980) (1) pp. 20–4.

Department of Education and Science, *Teacher Education and Training* (James Report) (London: HMSO, 1972)

S. Fisher and D. Hicks, *Planning Workshops and Courses: a World Studies In-Service Handbook* (Schools Council/Rowntree Project, World Studies 8–13, 1982)

D. Galloway, 'Learning from experience: a course for advisory teachers', *British Journal of In-Service Education*, 8 (1982) (3) pp. 177–80.

G. Haigh, 'Where there's Scope there's hope!', *Times Educational Supplement* (27 May 1977) p. 16.

J. L. Herman and J. P. Yeh, 'Some effects of parent involvement in schools', *Resources in Education* (1980) ED 206 963 (Abstract)

J. Hewison, 'Parental involvement in the teaching of reading', *Remedial Education*, 17 (1982) (4) pp. 156–62.

J. Hewison, 'The Haringey Project': summary in B. Tizard, J. Mortimore and

B. Burchell, *Involving Parents in Nursery and Infant Schools: a Source Book for Teachers* (London: Grant McIntyre, 1980)

J. Hewison and J. Tizard, 'Parental involvement and reading attainment', *British Journal of Educational Psychology*, 50 (1980) pp. 209–15.

M. Knowles, *The Adult Learner: A Neglected Species* (Gulf Publishing Co., 1977)

R. Long, *Involving Parents in Early Childhood Education – Development of a School-Focused In-Service Course for Teachers* (University of Sheffield: M. Ed. dissertation, 1983)

P. Lyons *et al.*, 'Involving Parents – a Handbook for Participation in Schools', report paper from *Resources in Education* (1983) ED 219 851.

S. T. Parnes and A. Meadow, 'Effect of brainstorming instructions on creative problem-solving by trained and untrained subjects', *Journal of Educational Psychology*, 50 (1959) pp. 171–6.

A. M. Pope, 'The teacher as learner – some factors in the learning process', *British Journal of In-Service Education*, 7 (1980) (1) pp. 70–6.

M. Prosser, 'The myth of parental apathy', *Times Educational Supplement* (16 Oct. 1981) pp. 22–3.

T. Smith, *Parents and Preschool* (London: Grant McIntyre, 1980)

B. Tizard, 'No common ground', *Times Educational Supplement* (27 May 1977) pp. 15–16.

B. Tizard, W. N. Schofield and J. Hewison, 'Collaboration between teachers and parents in assisting children's reading', *British Journal of Educational Psychology*, 52 (1982) pp. 1–15.

P. Widlake and F. MacLeod, *Raising Standards* (Coventry: Community Education Development Centre, 1984)

E. C. Wragg, *Teaching Teaching* (Newton Abbot: David and Charles, 1974)